Happening Hanukkah

CREATIVE WAYS TO CELEBRATE

KITCHEN APPLIANCES AND SCISSORS ARE NOT TOYS AND SHOULD BE USED CAREFULLY.
THE ACTIVITIES DESCRIBED IN THIS BOOK WHICH REQUIRE COOKING, PAINTING, OR CUTTING
SHOULD ONLY BE PERFORMED UNDER ADULT SUPERVISION OR WITH AN ADULT'S PERMISSION.

For Jody Kabat Gelfand (Madeline G.'s, Erica G.'s and Jessica G.'s exceptional mom)

Many thanks to my editor, Emily Sollinger, for her thoughtful comments and guidance;
and thank you to Wendy Malkin Broudy and Sandra Gutierrez for their love, support, and coffee.

J 394.267 Z ~ D.m

Text copyright © 2002 by Debra Mostow Zakarin. Illustrations copyright © 2002 by Amanda Haley.
All rights reserved. Published by Grosset & Dunlap, a division of Penguin Putnam
Books for Young Readers, 345 Hudson Street, New York, NY 10014. GROSSET & DUNLAP is a
trademark of Penguin Putnam Inc. Published simultaneously in Canada. Printed in the U.S.A.

ISBN 0-448-42869-5   A B C D E F G H I J

Happening Hanukkah

CREATIVE WAYS TO CELEBRATE

BY DEBRA MOSTOW ZAKARIN
ILLUSTRATED BY AMANDA HALEY

Grosset & Dunlap • New York

HAPPY HANUKKAH

It's Hanukkah! Let's celebrate! If you think Hanukkah is just about the story of the Macabees, lighting the menorah, or giving kisses to your old Aunt Estelle after she gives you yet another pair of itchy crocheted socks, then think again!

Hanukkah is about fun, family, and friends. It is about giving and receiving, laughter and excitement. It is about playing games, cooking and eating great food, presents, decorations, and amazing parties. When else do you get to have fun for eight nights straight with terrific people you like hanging with? When else do you get to decorate the house from top to bottom and celebrate old and new traditions?

After you're through with this book, you'll be sure to have the best and most happening Hanukkah. You'll learn how to throw an awesome Hanukkah party complete with

great eats, fun games and cool party favors, make edible menorahs and dreidels (lip-smacking good!), and, create and design groovy gifts like Hanukkah earrings, lunchbox purses, and friendship bracelets.

Not only will you learn how to make the yummiest *latkes* (aka potato pancakes), and design and decorate fabulous frames, you'll also learn the true meaning of Hanukkah and why we light the menorah.

Each night can be a different opportunity to give and receive. On the first night you can exchange store-bought gifts. On the second night you can exchange homemade gifts (great ideas just pages away). On the third night have a grab bag, and on the fourth night bring a basket of food and canned goods to your nearest shelter. Need some ideas for the fifth, sixth, seventh, and eighth nights? Read on! It's all here. Remember, whatever you choose to do, do it together. Hanukkah is meant to be shared with friends and family.

Well, what are you waiting for? Turn the page and start having a very happening and happy Hanukkah!

THE STORY OF HANUKKAH

Hanukkah begins on the 25th of Kislev on the Hebrew calendar. On our calendar, Hanukkah usually falls at the end of November or in December.

In Hebrew, the word *Hanukkah* means "dedication." Hanukkah celebrates the rededication of the holy Temple in Jerusalem after the Jewish people defeated Antiochus, the Greek King of Syria. Antiochus outlawed Jewish rituals. He wanted everyone, including the Jews, to worship Greek Gods the way he did.

The Jewish people got angry when Antiochus seized their holy Temple. The Jews rebelled, and fighting began in *Modi'in*, a village near Jerusalem.

Mattathias, a Jewish High Priest (nowadays, Mattathias would be known as the Rabbi of his village), gathered his five sons and other Jewish villagers to defend their right to practice their religious beliefs and rituals. A year after the fighting began, Mattathias died.

But before his death he put his brave son Judah Maccabee in charge of their growing army. After three years of fighting, the Jews defeated the Greek army, even though they had fewer men and weapons.

Judah Maccabee and his fighters returned to their holy Temple. They had a big dedication ceremony. For the celebration, the Maccabees (all the Jewish fighters were now called Maccabees in honor of their brave leader, Judah) wanted to light a candelabrum, called a menorah, to celebrate. They looked everywhere for oil to burn but only found a small flask that contained enough oil to light the menorah for one night. Miraculously, the oil lasted for eight days. This gave the Maccabees enough light and time to find fresh oil for their treasured menorah of the Temple that they loved.

Today, Jews everywhere around the world celebrate Hanukkah for eight days and nights. They light candles in a menorah every night, remembering the eight-day miracle and the rededication of the holy Temple. They also remember and respect the right to practice all religious beliefs freely.

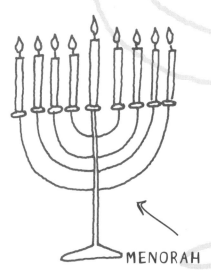
MENORAH

CRAFTY & HIP HANUKKAH GIFTS

Let's be honest here. Wouldn't you agree that giving and receiving gifts is one of the most fun parts of Hanukkah? Who doesn't like to wildly tear off wrapping paper and rip open a

box to find the sweater they've been eyeing for the past few months or the hottest new game that everyone seems to be getting this year? Sure, store-bought gifts are great! But when you get right down to it, your piggy bank may not be as large as you remembered it to be and there are so many

SAM

friends and family you want to give gifts to. If you don't want to break the bank and you also want to bring a personal touch to your Hanukkah celebration, then make your own nifty gifts to give.

So go on, roll up your sleeves, and let's begin crafting.

Many of the materials and objects needed for these crafts can be found at your local craft store!

COOL COUPONS!

Can't figure out what to buy or make for that hard-to-give-to someone? Have no fear—Hanukkah Coupons are good for here, there, and everywhere. You can make a whole bunch of individual coupons and give them out to many different people as gifts, or you can make a whole booklet for one extraordinary someone.

CREATIVE COUPONS

You can put as many or as few coupons in each booklet for each night. Just make sure not to include or give out too many, because this is one gift people are sure to "cash in."

Think really hard about the person you will give the coupons to. What does that person really like to do and what would you like to do with them or for them?

Your booklets can have a theme, such as:

- Beauty
- Sports
- Movie Madness
- Around the House
- Let's Eat
- Going Green (gardening or recycling activities)

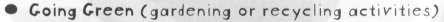

Or, the booklets can include a variety of services, such as:

- A manicure or pedicure
- Rainy day video watching fest at your place (complete with videos and munchies)
- Breakfast in bed
- Home-style car wash
- Organizing your brother's room
- Making your sister's bed every day for a week
- Scorekeeper and caddy at your mom or dad's next golf game

COUPONS CONTINUED...

The more creative you are the more fun you and the recipient will have. You can get really into the spirit of the holiday and make Hanukkah-themed coupons;

Homemade *latke* dinner for two

Hanukkah solo concert—featuring songs sung by you (Grandparents will *totally* get into this one)

"Good for One" basket of *sufganiyot*—to be redeemed any time after Hanukkah. (Once you taste *sufganiyot* (sweet, jelly-filled dough-nuts) you won't be able to wait a whole year until Hanukkah to have more!)

Here's what you need:

8½ x 11 inch sheet of card stock paper
    (one sheet will make eight coupons)
Scissors
Colored pens and pencils
Ruler
Glitter, paint, stickers, rhinestones and rubber stamps
Hole punch
Ribbon

Here's what you do:

- With a ruler, divide the paper in half lengthwise and cut.

- Next, divide and cut these two long pieces in half across their width and in half again to make eight equal rectangles.

- On each rectangle write in fancy lettering a "gift" or "service" from you to the recipient

- Decorate each coupon with glitter, stickers, paint, and anything you think will look totally cool. For example, if one of the coupons is a manicure, then draw a picture of a hand and paint the nails with real polish!

- Hole-punch the coupons along the left side, thread with thin ribbon, and tie in a bow.

NOT JUST ANY FRIENDSHIP BRACELET

Besides being there for side-aching giggles and late night sleepover chats or sharing the back of your sleeve during a super emotional runny-nose cry, there is no better way to show your best friends just how much they mean to you than by giving each of them a friendship bracelet. Even when you're not together, all your friends have to do is look down at their wrists to know that you're thinking of them.

Here's what you need:

Three 48 inch strands of **embroidery thread,** in three different colors. You can also use yarn, silk cord, or plastic lanyard.

Tape

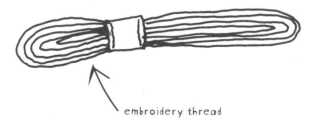

embroidery thread

Here's what you do:

1. Hold the embroidery thread (or whatever type of yarn you are using) strands together so that they are lined up evenly.

2. Fold the bunch of thread in half. Now, tie an overhand knot one inch from the fold, creating a loop.

3. Tape the knot to a table.

4. You will now have 2 strands of each color. Separate them into three groups— each of the same color.

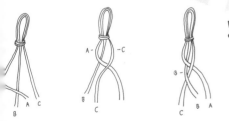

5. Now, begin braiding the three groups together. Braid repeatedly until the bracelet is as long as you'd like. Tie the loose ends together with a knot.

6. Now, slip the ends through the loop at the opposite end of the braid, tie a knot to secure the bracelet, and trim the ends.

15

A REASON FOR FLOWERS

Who doesn't like to receive flowers? Nobody I know! However, did you ever notice how no one can ever find a vase? Look no further. These **glass vases** make great Hanukkah gifts as well as great party decorations.

Here's what you need:

Acrylic or liquid tempera paints
White glue
Clear glass jar (You can find one at the craft store or use an empty jelly, jam, or juice jar with the jar washed and dried and the label peeled off. To really get into the spirit of the holiday, use an empty olive oil bottle.
Paintbrushes
Clear liquid glaze (You can find this at the craft store. This glaze "waterproofs" the paint and gives your design a nice shine.)

Here's what you do:

- In order to make the paints stick to the glass, mix each of the colors with some glue.
- Keep the paint thick so it won't run.
- Paint any design you want on the jar.
- Let the jar dry.
- Seal the finished design by brushing on a coat of clear liquid glaze.

There are so many neat designs you can paint on your vase; flowers, person's name (Hebrew or English) or initials, polka dots, faces, clowns, tennis ball and racquet, volleyballs, and even animals. Or stick with the Hanukkah theme and paint a Star of David, a Menorah, or dreidels.

If you'd like your vase to have some texture, glue on buttons, rhinestones, beads, sequins, or fabric, and then apply the clear liquid glaze.

COOKING IS AN ART

For a totally funky gift, make an unusual **apron** for the cook in your family. Your design can be abstract or have a theme such as: flowers, interpretive portraits of everyone in your family with their mouths open and saying, "Feed Us Now!", an American Flag (for those Fourth-of-July barbeques), and even a Hanukkah theme complete with menorah and dreidel.

Do you have a grandparent who likes to cook or bake? Then get all the grandkids together and have everyone dip his or her hands in paint (a different color for each grandchild) and then press them on to the apron. If you don't want to paint anything on the apron, then write some funny sayings such as- "Don't complain to the cook. . . it could be liver," "Kiss the Cook!", or "#1 Chef."

Here's what you need:

White or off-white apron (This can be found at a craft store or department store.)

Fabric paints or pens (Only use fabric paints because other kinds of paint will come off in the wash.)

Paper plates

Here's what you do:

- Lay the apron right side up
- Pour each different color of fabric paint onto a different paper plate (this will keep your workspace more organized.)
- Now, with your design in mind—go to it! (Or, first sketch it out with a pencil on a piece of paper!)
- With the fabric pen, sign your name at the bottom or even at the end of one of the ties. (All great artists sign their work—and you are one of them!)
- Let the paint dry (it will take about one day.)

Not quite sure that painting on the apron is the way you want to go? Then sew on your design with groovy iron-on appliqués, patches, sequins, buttons and even flashy rhinestones.

Here's another idea: if you don't know any chefs then turn this cook's apron into an "artist smock."

ARE YOU GAME?

Games are a great gift to give anyone at any age. This **Magnetic Tic Tac Toe Game Box** is sure to be a hit, and can make a great party favor (especially if you use mini boxes). Your mom can play with it to relax on her business trip, your dad can play while waiting to pick you up from karate class, and your brother and sister can play in the backseat of the car during a family road trip. (This will keep them from bugging you!)

Here's what you need:

Paper boxes with lids (such as a shoe box, sweater box, or small gift box)

Acrylic paints (three different colors of your choice)

Craft glue

Ten small round magnets

Magnetic paint (These paints are so cool because they turn any paintable surface into a magnetic surface. Infused with iron dust, this non-toxic magnetic paint works as a primer that attracts magnets. After the paint dries your surface is magnetic).

Pencil

Ruler

Ten ⅜-inch wooden buttons

All of the above can be found at your craft store and hardware store.

Here's what you do:

- Paint the outside top and underneath of the lid with magnetic paint. Let it dry.

Note: The more coats of magnetic paint you apply the more receptive to magnets the box will be, but don't go crazy (two or three coats are just fine).

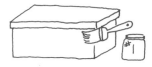

- Paint the outside edges of the lid and all four outsides of the box with acrylic paint color #1. When the magnetic paint is completely dry, paint the top of the lid with acrylic paint color #1.

3. Paint five wooden buttons with acrylic paint color #2 and five wooden buttons with acrylic paint color #3.

4. When the paint on the buttons is completely dry, glue small round magnets to the bottom of each button.

5. With a thin paintbrush, add the tic-tac-toe lines to the top of the lid with color #2 or #3.

If you're feeling really motivated about designing a magnetic game, then try your hand at a checkerboard or chess set.

21

NOT JUST FOR LUNCH!

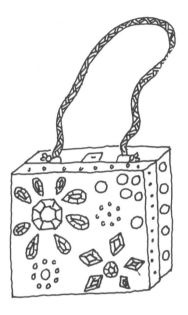

Hey, trendsetter! The only problem you'll have with this gift is you won't want to give it up. Trust me! Depending on your design, these **jeweled purse lunchboxes** can be used as an everyday purse for your hippest gal pal, as an evening bag for your mom, as a makeup box for that friend or family member on the go, or as a super-funky lunchbox.

These jeweled purse boxes also make a great arts-and-crafts holder for your buttons and sequins; a box to hold letters and cards from friends and family; or a place to store special keepsakes. (What best friend wouldn't love this?)

Here's what you'll need:

Acrylic jewels in different shapes, sizes, and colors
Tiny glass marbles
Satin cord or thick ribbon
White double-sided adhesive sticky paper
Glue
Small or large metal lunchbox (Don't worry if there is a design on it—you'll be decorating over it.)
Pencil
Ruler
Scissors
Tape
Tweezers

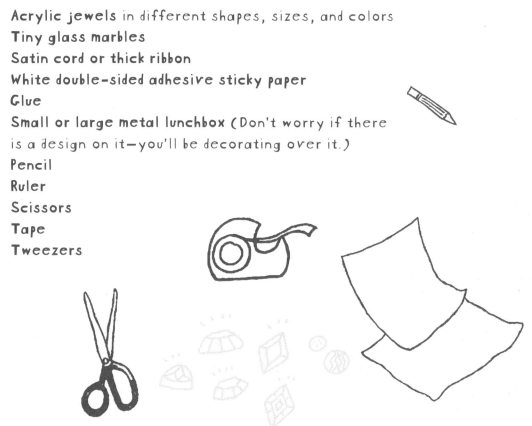

Here's what you do:

- On a piece of paper, sketch out a design for the purse. Your design can be carefree and random, or it can have a specific motif such as: roses, the Star of David, beauty items (like lipstick and nail polish bottles), or a globe. This sketch will serve as your "guide" when gluing on the jewels.

- Once your design is sketched out (for the front, back, top, bottom and sides of the lunchbox), measure the front of the lunchbox. Cut the white double-sided adhesive sticky paper to fit the front of the box.

- Peel off the backing and carefully place it on top of box. (Don't worry if you can see the picture that's already on the metal lunch box—you won't be able to see it once the jewels are glued on.)

- Peel the top protective layer off to reveal adhesive. (This top side will eventually be fully covered with the jewels.)

- Using your pencil design as a guide, place a dab of glue on the bottom side of the acrylic jewel and then carefully place it on the adhesive tape. (Even though you're using double-sided adhesive white paper, the glue will reinforce the jewels even more.) For hard-to-reach places, use the tweezers.
  If there are any exposed places, use tiny glass marbles to

"fill" in these spots—so that the adhesive won't be visible. The idea is to cover the entire box with jewels.

- Repeat the above process for the back and all the sides of the lunchbox.

- With your scissors, cut the plastic handle off of the lunchbox.

- Take the satin cord or ribbon and tie tightly to the metal handle loops. To make the satin strap or ribbon even more interesting, use two or three different colors, braid them, and then attach the braid to the metal handle loops.

Work slowly and carefully, and on one section at a time when making this lunchbox purse. As a variation, you can use buttons, beads, sequins, or even stickers.

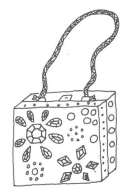

GET FRAMED!

Picture Frames are so much fun to make, to give and to receive. You can get really creative and think of the personality and interests of the person who will be receiving this amazing gift. Do you have a friend or family member who is just nuts about felines or has a temper like a tiger? Then this leopard photo frame will be fabulously received and is quite fast to make!

Here's what you need:

Craft glue

Ruler

5 x 7 inch clear acrylic or wood photo frame

Scissors

Faux leopard-fur trim

(You can find this at your craft store or at a fabric store.)

Here's what you do:

- Measure about ½ inch around each side of the frame.
- Cut the faux leopard-fur trim to cover that ½ inch all around, leaving a bit of excess to bend behind the edges.
- Carefully, working on one side at a time, glue the fur trim onto the border of the frame as well as to the back.
- Let the frame dry completely.

PICTURE THIS... Got a friend who is into glam? Buy some fake nails at the beauty store, polish them in all different funky colors and designs, and glue them on to the frame. If your family just returned from a remarkable cross-country trip then cut up a map and make a travel frame collage. For all these frame ideas, add some sheen by painting on a coat of clear liquid glaze.

By the way, buttons, bottle caps, beads, rhinestones and small marbles also make for awesome frame designs. You can even place a photo of you and the recipient in the frame for that extra personal touch.

PICTURE PERFECT

Jazz up a photo of you and a pal with beads, small tiles, or funky buttons and suddenly you've got the coolest **picture mosaic!** You can either use one type of medium (such as tiles or beads) or all of them for the photo.

Here's what you need:

Variety of beads, small tiles, or funky buttons in different colors, shapes, and sizes
A favorite photo
Glue
Tweezers
Cardboard

Here's what you do:

- First, take the photo to your local copy center and color copy it to a larger size—like, 8 ½ x 11 or even 11 x 17.

- At home, lay the picture on a flat surface.

- Begin to glue the beads, small tiles, or funky buttons on top of the picture (you will be completely covering the photo). Choose beads that match the colors in the photo (red hair— red beads).

- For large areas of the same color, place a thin layer of glue over the area and then press on the beads.

- For smaller details, place a little dot of glue on the individual bead and place it on the photo. For those hard-to-reach spots, use tweezers.

- Once all the beads have been glued to the photo, let it dry completely.

- When it's dry, glue the completed mosaic to the cardboard. You don't have to use a photo—cool magazine pictures work well, too!

BEAD IT!

Okay, accessory goddess, these Hanukkah earrings will keep you in the holiday spirit all day long and night as they swing from your lobes. But beware! Each of your fashion-frenzied friends is going to demand a pair! Lucky for you, they are super fun and fast to make (once you get the hang of it)!

Here's what you need:

Different colored beads
Earring wires
Earring hangers or fasteners
(All of the above can be found at the craft store)

Here's what you do:

1. Take four pieces of wire, each about 2 ½ inches long. Carefully bend two of the wires into the shape of a triangle.

2. String each wire with with beads of any color you desire. (Be patient; it gets a bit tricky around the corners).

3. Take a straight wire (that has been beaded) and weave it in and out of the triang shaped wire, bending the straight wire into a triang shape too. Now you have made a Star of David!

4. Repeat the same for the other two pieces of wire.

5. Attach the star to the earring hanger.

Since you've got all these beads, why not thread them on to some thin yarn or string and make some funky bracelets? You can even make super-cool name bracelets with letter beads, and heart bracelets with different heart-shaped beads.

Because holiday time is also the time to give, invite your friends over after school one day and make a whole bunch of **heart bracelets**. Instead of exchanging gifts with family one Hanukkah evening, make these bracelets together. Then, visit your local retirement or nursing home and see how many smiles you get when you give these heart bracelets as gifts to those who will really appreciate it. (This also makes a great gift for your Hebrew-school teacher.)

SNUGGLE UP!

There is no better way to warm up during Hanukkah than in a cozy menorah sweatshirt. Paint a menorah with your kid brother's favorite cartoon characters as the candle holders or design an ABC menorah for your favorite younger cousin. You can find lots of inexpensive sweatshirts at most clothing stores (check the sale rack) and even at many craft stores.

Here's what you need:

Sweatshirt (preferably white or a very light color)
Paper
Pencil
Piece of cardboard (about 11 x 17)
Fabric Paints (don't use any other kind; they will come off in the wash)

Here's what you do:

- Prewash and dry the sweatshirt.

- Design your menorah, on a piece of paper.

- Place the cardboard in between the front and back of the sweatshirt (this will keep the paints from soaking through.)

- With the fabric paints, using the paper design as your guide, you are now a fashion designer.

- If you want to decorate the back of the sweatshirt, make sure to wait until the front design is completely dry.

This makes a great gift for any person at any age. You don't have to paint a menorah; you can design anything you like, such as a Hebrew name on the front and an English name on the back, dreidels, and anything else you can think of. This will also work on **T-shirts**, caps, socks, or underwear...go **crazy**, style queen!

DO IT WRITE!

There is one gift you can never have enough of . . . a journal! Journals can be used in so many different ways: as a secret diary, to practice your story-writing skills, as an artist sketchpad, or as a place to jot down your favorite song lyrics or even what Hanukkah means to you.

Here's what you need:

A plain journal (with or without lines)
Glue
Various **decorative items**, such as: beads, buttons, magazine pictures, photos, a cut-up map, and anything else you can think of.

Here's what you do:

Think about the person who will be receiving this journal. Is it a travel journal for your favorite jet-setter Aunt? Then go wild with the map. Is it a music journal for a rock 'n roll obsessed cousin? Plaster the journal with magazine photos of awesome guitars.

For even more of a personal touch, write a friendship quote or saying on the first page.

You can even make this into a Hanukkah journal completely adorned with dreidels and Hanukkah candles. Then, during Hanukkah, you and your family can go around the room and write down what you're thankful for or a favorite Hanukkah memory. Every year, crack open the journal and read it aloud. Have your thoughts and feelings changed or evolved over the year? This is sure to be a treasured keepsake for your whole family!

THOUGHTFUL ACTS OF KINDNESS

Your list of people to give gifts to may be long, but it always feels good to give gifts to those who probably least expect it and who really need it. Choose a local organization (such as a women's or homeless shelter) or a national charity, and make somebody's holiday that much happier. Design your own charity box and collect money throughout the year. (Did you know that the Hebrew word for **"charity"** is **tzedakah**?)

When it's Hanukkah, break open the box and give to the charity or organization you picked.

Here's what you need:

- Empty cardboard milk or juice carton (either small or large)
- Construction paper
- Scissors
- Markers, crayons, buttons, sequins, stickers, beads, or anything you can think of for decorations.
- Double-sided tape
- Glue
- Hole punch
- Ribbon

Here's what you do:

- Open out the top of the carton and wash it carefully. Dry it completely.

- Wrap construction paper around the carton and cut to fit, leaving a little bit of overlap at the top and bottom.

- With a pencil, lightly mark the corners of the carton.

- Remove the paper and fold along the pencil lines you just drew.

- Using markers, crayons, buttons, and anything else you can think of, decorate the paper any way you please.

- Glue and tape the paper back around the carton.

- Cut a small slit (large enough for coins) on the top of one side of the carton.

- Fold the carton top together and punch two holes in it.

- Run ribbon through the holes and tie the carton closed.

MENORAH MADNESS!

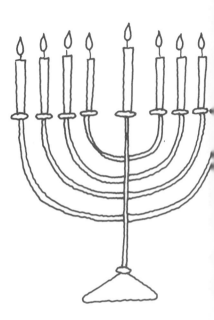

Some families don't just light one menorah. In many houses, every family member gets to light their own menorah. It's also nice to keep a couple of extra ones around the house for friends who are visiting. Menorahs come in all different shapes and sizes. The one thing that they all have in common is nine stems—one for each of the eight nights, plus the *shamash*. The shamash can be anywhere on the menorah—it just has to be a bit taller than all the other stems. Why the shamash? In Hebrew, shamash means "service." The eight candles are supposed to be lit for the sole purpose of remembering the miracle. Therefore, the ninth candle (the *shamash*) is used to light each of these candles.

For a great family activity one night after lighting the candles, make one of these neat menorahs together.

WOODEN MENORAH

Here's what you need:

A wooden base
9 metal bottle caps
A hammer
Acrylic paints
9 nails

Here's what you do:

● The base can be a wooden plank, board, or slat. It can be a wooden sculpture made of pieces of wood glued or hammered together—be as creative with the design as you'd like.

● Sand your wooden base until it's as smooth as you can get it. (if you like, shellac it or paint on a design)

● Lay out the bottle caps along the wooden base with the rough edges facing up.

● Carefully nail the bottle caps to the base.

● Set the candles on top of the caps (to get the candles to stay, you may have to light the candles and drip some wax on the caps, the stick on the candles before the wax hardens.)

This next menorah really uses all the symbols of Hanukkah; menorah, light (candles) and a potato. That's right, a potato.

POTATO MENORAH

Here's what you need:

Potato
Knife
9 Hanukkah candles

Here's what you do:

● Cut a large baking potato in half the long way.

● Cut a flat slice off the bottom for it to stand (so that it won't wobble around).

● Use the tip of a knife to dig out candle-size holes (birthday candles wor really well with this kind of menorah.)

● Don't forget, the shamash needs to be taller than all the rest of the candles, so don't dig out as deep of a hole for it.

This menorah also makes a cute table decoration.

Really get into the spirit of Hanukkah and eat this edible menorah for lunch during one of the eight days.

EDIBLE MENORAH

Here's what you need:

Slice of bread (whatever kind you prefer)
Peanut butter (cream cheese also will work just fine)
Thin stick pretzels
Golden raisins

Here's what you do:

Spread a thin layer of peanut butter on one side of the bread.
Design a menorah out of the thin stick pretzels.
Place golden raisins above the thin stick pretzels for the flames.

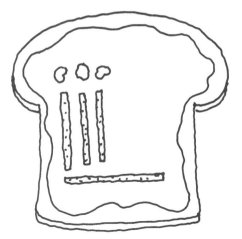

THE ULTIMATE HANUKKAH PARTY

What would be the coolest way to gather together all your friends to celebrate Hanukkah? Throw the ultimate bash complete with fab food, games, and party favors.

Before you start sending out the invites or calling everyone up to save the date, make sure to clear it with the folks first. In fact, why not throw the party with them? They can have some of their friends and you can have some of yours (this might even help with the cost). Once you've got the parental go-ahead, make a list of everyone you'd like to invite. The amount of people you invite will also depend on how much money you have to spend.

There is no right or wrong time to have a Hanukkah party—as long as it's during Hanukkah, of course. Check your calendar and find out exactly when Hanukkah will be (remember, it changes from year to year). Decide whether you want to have the party in the afternoon or evening, and during the week or on a weekend day.

Once you've set the date for the party, make sure to keep the details straight with this checklist.

You will need:

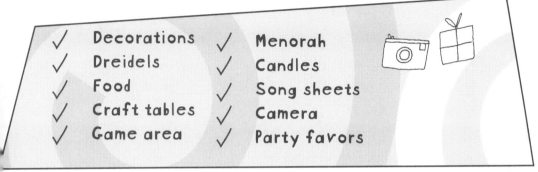

- ✓ Decorations
- ✓ Dreidels
- ✓ Food
- ✓ Craft tables
- ✓ Game area
- ✓ Menorah
- ✓ Candles
- ✓ Song sheets
- ✓ Camera
- ✓ Party favors

Great! Now that all the specifics of what you'll need are in order, let's begin.

Wait one sec. Before we go on, please be aware that many of the mouthwatering recipes in this book require the use of oven, microwave, stove, and sharp utensils. Make sure to always be super-careful and ask a grown-up for permission and help.

And one last thing: many of the ingredients needed for these recipes can be found at your local supermarket.

Now, we can begin. Let's party!

FESTIVE FEAST

You can serve many different kinds of food at your happening Hanukkah party. Many of the foods we eat at Hanukkah are traditional foods from Israel. Just like we can buy a hamburger and fries at almost any corner in the United States, the same can be said about Israel— except instead of a burger and fries it's pita pockets filled with falafel.

If you've never eaten falafel, you and your guests are in for a mouth-watering treat! Also sold on the streets of Israel, before and during Hanukkah, are sufganiyot—delicious jelly doughnuts. That is why falafel and sufganiyot are perfect to serve; they are deep-fried in oil. During Hanukkah, people eat lots of fried foods in celebration of the oil that lasted not one day, but eight days.

Hanukkah food traditions vary from home to home, but the one great dish that everyone serves (and loves) is latkes—

Hanukkah
Feast

potato pancakes. Latkes are also deep fried in oil, keeping with the Hanukkah tradition. It's because of the oil that we eat latkes year after year, not because Judah and the Macabees were eating potatoes on the battlefield, since potatoes weren't even available until the 16th century.

Starter
Hummus with Pita bread

Main Course
Falafel in Pita Pockets
Tabouli salad

Side Dishes
Potato Latkes
Zucchini Latkes
Apple Sauce
Sour Cream

Dessert
Sufganiyot
Marshmallow Dreidels

HANUKKAH RECIPES

HUMMUS

Ingredients you will need:

½ cup **tahini** (a scrumptious sauce made from sesame seed oil mixed with spicy seasoning. It usually comes in a glass jar and can be found in your supermarket)

⅓ cup **water** (or more)

¼ cup **olive oil**

6 tablespoons fresh **lemon juice**

4 cloves **garlic** (peeled)

3½ cups fresh **chickpeas**, dried and soaked. (Chickpeas are also known as garbanzo beans. You can use canned chickpeas, but fresh ones are a bit more flavorful.)

½ teaspoon **cumin**

1 teaspoon **coriander**

Salt and **pepper** to taste

Chopped **parsley**

Paprika

Here's what you do:

- If you do choose to use fresh chickpeas, place them in a pot, cover them completely in water and soak them overnight.
- Once the chickpeas have been soaked overnight, uncover them, bring them to a boil on the stove, lower the flame, and cook them for about two hours.
- After two hours of cooking, drain the chickpeas in a colander (a bowl with small holes) or a strainer.
- Combine the tahini, water, olive oil, lemon juice, and garlic in the food processor (or blender) and blend until smooth.
- Add the drained chickpeas, cumin and coriander. Add salt and pepper to taste and blend all the ingredients together.

To serve hummus Israeli-style, thinly spread it on a round plate and pour a small amount of olive oil (there it is again—oil!) in the center. Sprinkle the hummus with a small handful of chopped parsley, paprika, and chickpeas. Serve with small slices of pita bread. (Toast the pita slices for extra crunch!)

Tip: Before beginning any recipe have all of your ingredients out on the table. This will keep you organized.

FALAFEL BALLS

Ingredients you will need:

1 ounce can **chickpeas** (drained very well)

Water

3 **green onions**

½ cup **parsley sprigs**

4 cloves **garlic**

1 **egg**

1 teaspoon **ground cumin**

½ teaspoon **baking soda**

Salt and pepper

Oil for frying (any kind will do)

Here's what you do:

- Place chickpeas, green onions, parsley, garlic, egg, cumin, and a few dashes of salt and pepper in a food processor or blender.
- Process until almost smooth. Let stand 15 minutes. Place in refrigerat to chill.
- Once mixture is chilled, moisten your hands with a bit of water and pinc off pieces of the bean mixture (about ¾ inch in diameter). Shape into small balls with your hands.

● Fill a large pot with enough oil so that when you drop the falafel balls into it, they will be covered. Once the oil has been brought to a boil (bubbling), gently and carefully drop the falafel balls one by one into the oil using a large metal spoon. Deep fry in the hot oil until browned on all sides (about 2 to 3 minutes). Remove the falafel balls from the oil with a large slotted metal spoon and place on paper towels to drain off some of the excess oil.

Important: Never do this without an adult! The oil gets very hot very quickly—you could burn yourself. Always cook with caution and use good common sense.

Makes about 24 falafel balls. Stuff falafel balls into sliced pita pockets. Add shredded lettuce, chopped tomatoes, chopped onions, chopped pickles and olives. Drizzle with tahini sauce. Enjoy!

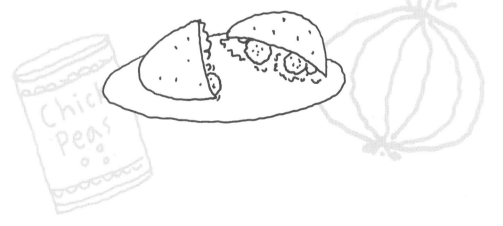

TABOULI SALAD

Ingredients you will need:

¾ cup **bulgur wheat** (Bulgur wheat is a scrumptious grain that can be found at your supermarket in the same aisle as rice.)

1 ½ cups **water**

1 pound **tomatoes**, chopped

¼ cup **olive oil**

4 tablespoons fresh **parsley**

1 teaspoon **salt**

½ **cucumber**, finely chopped

¼ cup **lemon juice**

2 cloves **garlic**, finely chopped

3 **green onions**, chopped

2 tablespoons **fresh mint**, choppe

Here's what you do:

● Pour the bulgur wheat and salt into a medium-size pot of boiling water.

● Turn off the flame and let it stand for about 20 minutes, until all the water is absorbed. The bulgur wheat is ready when it is soft and there is no more water in the pot.

● In a small bowl, mix together the olive oil, parsley, lemon juice, garlic, and mint. Pour it over the bulgur wheat and gently mix it all together.

● Leave the mixture in a cool place for two hours, or in the refrigerator overnight.

● Before serving, add the tomatoes, cucumbers, and green onions. Mix it all together.

Serves about 6 people.

ngredients you will need:

1½ pounds **baking potatoes**, peeled

1 medium **onion**, chopped

1 **egg,** lightly beaten

1 teaspoon **salt**

¼ teaspoon **pepper**

2 tablespoons **flour**

½ teaspoon **baking powder**

Oil for frying

(Any kind of oil will do, but olive oil has such a great taste to it.)

Iere's what you do:

● Grate the potatoes (with a hand grater or food processor) and place in a colander or strainer.

● Squeeze out as much of the moisture as you can from the potatoes by pushing down on the potatoes with a spoon or the palm of your hand.

● In a large bowl, combine the potatoes with the onion, egg, salt, pepper, flour, and baking powder.

● Heat ¼ cup of oil in a large frying pan until it's very hot.

- Carefully drop about 2 to 3 tablespoons of the potato mixture into the pan for each latke. This will make medium-sized latkes. (If you like your latkes super=big, then drop in larger amounts of the potato mixture.)
- Use the back of the spoon to flatten the potato mixture.
- Fry over medium heat for about 4 to 5 minutes per side (or until golden brown).
- Drain latkes on a paper towel.
- If necessary, add more oil to the frying pan for each batch. Serve warm with applesauce and sour cream on the side.

Makes about 16 latkes

To make zucchini latkes use all of the same ingredients and follow the same steps as the potatoes latkes except substitute the potatoes with 3 medium zucchini!

Not only are these dreidels easy to make and great-tasting, but they also make very cute table decorations when you haphazardly scatter them around the table.

Here's what you need:

Bag of large marshmallows
Red and black licorice sticks, cut into 1-inch pieces
Chocolate kiss candies (one for each marshmallow)
Toothpicks
Food coloring

Here's what you do:

- Take your toothpick and stick it into an unwrapped chocolate kiss candy, point side down.
- Slide the marshmallow into the toothpick so that it sits on top of the chocolate kiss candy.
- Next, slide the 1-inch piece of licorice on top of the marshmallow.
- If you'd like, dip another toothpick into the food coloring and write a Hebrew letter on each side of the marshmallow.

When eating these marshmallow dreidels—don't forget to remove the toothpicks!

LET THE GAMES BEGIN!

Games are a great way to entertain your guests at your happening Hanukkah bash. Set up games in different corners of the room and have your guests rotate from one corner to another. Or, if you're not having a party, play different games with your family after lighting the menorah. You can play games instead of, or in addition to, exchanging gifts.

Hanukkah just would not be Hanukkah without the fun game of dreidel.

The four letters on the dreidel are:

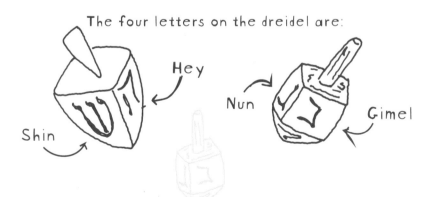

Hey

Shin

Nun

Gimel

In English these letters mean "A Great Miracle Happened There." This refers to the miracle of the oil lasting not one but eight nights.

PLAYING DREIDEL

Here's what you need:

At least **two players**
A dreidel
Pennies (if you're brave or feeling lucky, use nickels or dimes)
(Don't want to play for money? Try chocolate coins, beads, flavored lip glosses, nail polish bottles, gel pens, or even pieces of candy.)

Here's how you play:

- Divide the coins evenly between the players and the pot.
- Taking turns from left to right, one player spins the dreidel.
- When the dreidel stops, the player takes (or puts back) the coins according to which letter is facing up.

> Nun = Nothing happens
> Gimel = the player takes everything in the pot
> Hey = the player takes half the pot
> Shin = the player must put one coin into the pot

- Whoever has all the money (or candy) at the end wins—(and gets to keep it!)

GELT IN A BOWL

Here's what you need:

A bowl

10 coins for each player

Here's what you do:

- Place a bowl on the floor. Use a metal or plastic bowl—not glass.
- Each player begins with 10 coins—real or chocolate.
- Next, everyone lines up a few steps back from the bowl.
- Take turns tossing the coins into the bowl.
- Make it harder and harder each round by standing farther back from the bowl or by throwing with the opposite hand.
- The person to get the most coins in the bowl wins all the coins or even a special prize.

IT'S ALL IN THE WRIST!

Need a game that everyone at any age will enjoy?
Then **It's All in the Wrist** is for you!

Here's what you need:

Dreidel
Stopwatch

Here's what you do:

- Each player spins the dreidel once, and the spinning time is recorded.
- The winner of the contest is the player with the longest spinning record. (For a variation, you can try spinning the dreidel upside-down.)

After lighting the menorah, divide up into teams (such as: kids versus grown-ups). The team that loses has to clean the dinner dishes.

PERFECT PARTY MEMORIES!

There are some truly awesome ways to remember your happening Hanukkah party.

- Take lots of photos. Put them in an album and write funny captions beneath them.

- Put out some fabric markers and have your guests sign-in on a white T-shirt, pillowcase, or sheet.

- Set up a piece of poster board and pens, crayons, and markers and have your guests sign-in and draw a cool design for you to have forever and ever.

ET YOUR VOICE BE HEARD

You've practiced enough in the shower. Now it's time for everyone to hear your fresh voice. On Hanukkah, there are many songs to sing. Songs and dances (make up your own wild and funky steps) traditionally come after the lighting of the candles. Make sure to make enough copies of the song sheets for your party guests. And, remember, you don't need a party to sing and dance. Make it a tradition in your own house to let your voices be heard and get your feet grooving every night after lighting the menorah. If you're not sure of what some of the tunes are you can always buy a Hanukkah CD and sing along.

Hanukkah Song Sheet

OH, HANUKKAH

Oh, Hanukkah, Oh, Hanukkah,
Come light the menorah.
Let's have a party,
We'll all dance the hora.
Gather round the table,
We'll give you a treat.
Shining tops to play with,
And latkes to eat.
And while we are playing,
The candles are burning low.
One for each night,
They shed a sweet light,
To remind us of days long ago.

S'VIVON

S'vivon, sov, sov, sov,
Hanukkah hu chag tov
Hanukkah hu chag tov,
S'vivon sov, sov, sov
Chag simchah hu la'am,
Neis gadol hayah sham,
Chang simchah hu la'am
S'vivon turn, turn, turn,
While the lovely candles burn
What a great holiday,
Watch us sing and watch us play
Tell the story everywhere,
A great miracle happened there
It's a festival of lights
For eight days and for eight nights

LET THERE BE LIGHT!

A Hanukkah menorah is also called a *hanukkiyah*. The menorah has nine stems, one for each of the eight nights, and a center candle, called the *shamash*, which is used to light all the other candles.

Hanukkah candles are lit each night just after dark. On the first night, only one light is lit, the one at the far right, as you face the menorah. On the second night, when two lights are lit, the second one, the newest one, is lit first.

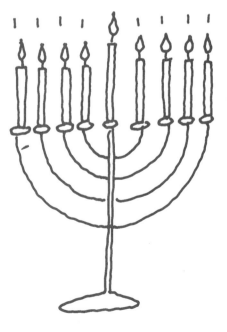

Inserting the candles into the menorah should be done in the reverse direction—from right to left. Therefore, on the eighth night, as you face the menorah, candles are placed into the menorah like this:

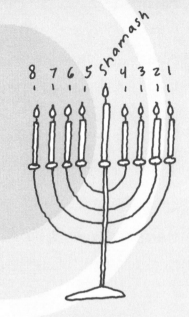

But, they are lit this way:
First, the *shamash* is lit and the following blessings are said:

Baruch at Adonai Elohainu melech ha'olam asher kidshanu b'mitzvotav v'tzivanu l'hadlik ner shel Chanukah.

Blessed are You, Lord or God, Ruler of
the universe, who has sanctified us with His
commandments and commanded us to kindle
the Chanukah light.

*Baruch ata Adonai Elohainu melech ha'olam sheh'asah
isim la'avotainu ba-yamim ha-hem bazman hazeh.*

Blessed are You, Lord our God, Ruler of
the Universe, Who has performed miracles
for our forefathers

And don't forget, the following blessing is
also recited but on the first night only:

*Baruch ata Adonai Elohainu melech ha'olam sheh'he-
cheh'yanu v'kiymanu v'higi'yanu lazman hazeh.*

Blessed are You, Lord our God, Ruler of
the universe, who has granted us life and
sustained us and brought us to this moment.

UNTIL NEXT YEAR

Remember the most happening part about celebrating Hanukkah is being with loved ones and setting up new traditions while keeping the old ones alive. There are so many cool ways to celebrate this awesome holiday besides exchanging gifts. Though, of course, that's fun too!

Spend time with friends and family, make homemade gifts and scrumptious foods, think about those who are not as fortunate a you, and don't forget about the Maccabees who fought for the right to practice one's own beliefs in freedom.

Until next year . . .

happy Hanukkah!

HAPPY HANUKKAH!